E. Harold Munn Jr.

1928–2016

PARTING THOUGHTS

AS TOLD TO
DANIEL V. RUNYON

E Harold Munn Jr. 1928-2016: *Parting Thoughts*
Copyright 2016 by Daniel V. Runyon

ISBN-13: 978-1530508563

Cover photo by Lifetouch Inc. Used by permission.

Publisher: Daniel V. Runyon
Spring Arbor, Michigan 49283
Print price: $11
eBook $6

This book is available online. Search Amazon.com: Daniel V. Runyon: Books

Contents

In all his serving, never for a moment did Hal Munn imagine he was earning his salvation—that was a gift he received from his Lord Jesus.

In all his serving, Hal Munn was obeying instructions given by Jesus in Matthew 22:37: "Love the Lord your God with all your heart and with all your soul and with all your mind."

1. Greenville

I was born Sept 7, 1928, in Vandalia, Fayette County, Illinois. They named me Junior because I was born on my parents' second wedding anniversary. We lived in Greenville, Illinois, but the nearest hospital was about 25 miles away in Vandalia.

My father was chair of the education department of Greenville College and director of the summer school. Mom taught English at Greenville and art in the public school, but her MA was in rhetoric from the University of Michigan. One of her students later became Bishop Boyd.

We lived in at least four different houses back in Greenville, and I think some of them were college-owned. The rent was part of my folks' salary because the college had no money, but I can recall my mother singing as she did the dishes.

I remember playing around her feet as she worked in the kitchen and hear her singing *Nothing but the Blood* and other very familiar gospel songs. Back in those days in church we sang out of the blue hymnal, and Leroy Melton would lead the singing. He never used a pitch pipe—he had a very good ear—and when you got those 350 people in Greenville all singing, now that was a sound to be heard!

The church had a fire, so we worshipped for some time in LaDue Auditorium, and I liked the seats there because they were opera seats that folded up, plus the wooden arm inserted over a metal track. I could slip them off and clap them together (not approved behavior).

A children's revival featured C. Dorr Demaray, future President of Seattle Pacific College (University). I was four years old, and I responded to the children's altar call. When I went home I bragged to Mother that I was saved. She said, "Oh, that's fine, Junior."

I replied, "Well, I'm only half saved." She said that was not an acceptable Christian condition. She prayed with me then and I made the profession of faith. I don't know if the "half-saved" notion was in reference to the salvation/sanctification language of the time, or what. They did test me as reading at the eighth grade level a year later when I was five, so maybe I had an advanced notion of some things. I began first grade at age four.

My father going to Greenville College as a student was an accident of association with a bunch of Free Methodist kids down the street, because he was headed for Asbury College as a Methodist Episcopal. But instead, he went to Greenville with the Baldwin tribe of kids, and there he met my mother who came from a Baptist background. She came to Greenville as a sophomore transferring from a small Baptist college in Osage, Iowa, that went belly-up.

My mother's family attended a Baptist church in Riceville that is still there, but Baptists at that time were undergoing growing pains and somehow got a modernist preacher in there, so my grandparents were not happy and went looking around. They found a little Free Methodist church with a young preacher just out of Greenville. He heard of Mother's plight and recommended that she attend Greenville. She did, and met my dad.

Dad was a leader on the debate team, he participated in student spiritual activities, and during the summers he sold typewriters and Bibles to pay his way through college. When he graduated in 1925 he got a job at Central College in Kansas, and Mom got a job at Wessington Springs in South Dakota, so they carried on their romance via two cent stamps for the year.

Dad helped organize the construction of Stoll Hall at Central College—he helped carry the cement and so forth. Greenville wanted to start a summer school and, for whatever reason, President Burritt reached out to Central and asked Dad to come back and start the summer school, which he did.

Mom and Dad came into Greenville on separate trains, were married at Greenville, and left for Dad's place at Central on the same train.

So my parents were people of great faith, and I guess I grew up to be very much like my father. I'm sure I had those usual teenage doubts on the way—I think that's a usual part of Christian growth—perhaps not for everybody, but it happened to be for me. But those doubts were erased.

I had the tendency of never ending up as necessarily the president or chairperson of groups I was involved with. I ended up as more of a facilitator, the same role Dad served in so many times in his career. If you wanted to get something facilitated, you'd get ahold of Earle Munn.

He was very active in the Prohibition Party and ran for president of the United States three different times. He ran in 1964 and did as well as Berry Goldwater—neither one got elected. Dad believed very strongly in principle. Claude Watson was one of his very important mentors, a

Free Methodist pastor turned attorney who rescued the FMC from bankruptcy in the 1930s.

During World War II when Hillsdale College enrollment cut back to 275 students (fewer than 20 male students), Dad took it upon himself to preach for almost three years at Osseo Freewill Baptist Church. I still have files of Dad's sermons. He worked them out very carefully.

He had his political talks as well as his sermons, and he was probably the only presidential candidate in 1964 to have campaigned totally on the east and west coast. When he gave his speeches in Times Square he got good coverage in the *New York Daily News.* The requirements were to have your own soapbox to stand on, your flag, and a pole and stand for the flag.

Dad would tell interesting, serious jokes. I remember him telling about Claude Watson, a fellow who was sent up here as supply bishop at a time when mini-skirts were coming into fashion and he said, "Well, I see the ladies are wearing their legs longer this year."

But getting back to my childhood in Greenville: I had just turned five years old when I started first grade, and by third grade I didn't know how to *print* because I could already write longhand. So the teacher had to check my papers because my classmates couldn't read my cursive handwriting.

At home I liked to pull an English literature book off the shelf and read, and Mom helped me with words I didn't know. Early on she showed me how to use a dictionary, and my dad has told me I was reading at a very advanced level in first grade, and I was younger than the other kids.

Some years ago I wrote down some childhood memories in a book intended for grandchildren. It would be fine if you wanted to insert that material here.

Childhood Memories

Did I ever get whippings? Yes—with a willow switch for not behaving in church. Games I played included kick-the can, roller skating on the sidewalks, monopoly, and chess.

I was given small birthday parties that included school friends. My favorite toys included a tractor set, a coaster wagon, a tricycle, and a bicycle bought with lawn mowing earnings.

There was no television yet when I was a child. We had no radio until I was about six, and then we listened selectively as a family, and I listened to children's programs mostly between 5 and 6:00 p.m. Radios then used tubes, not transistors. I recall programs involving Jack Armstrong, Tom Mix, Dick Tracy, Fred Allen, Amos & Andy, Lum & Abner, Easy Aces, Bank of America, and 64 Dollar Question.

My pets in Greenville consisted of a nanny goat, a large dog named Biff, and rabbits— primarily for meat. My best friend was Charles Cook, a boy from a very poor family on the next block. I understand he may have been killed in military service in World War II.

As a teen, my best friend was Jim Moench in Hillsdale, an excellent photographer and great assistant projector operator. Jim and I could pick most of the locks in the high school, but we used this talent only in connection with our sound system and projection work—it saved having to get a key from the principal or chief custodian.

My first memory of an automobile was a Ford Model A. It could average 30 mph and usually two flat tires on the 450 mile drive to visit my grandparents in either Ohio or Iowa.

I rode a train alone at age eight to Iowa to visit my grandparents, and at age nine in Chicago I rode the "el" with Dad when he attended Northwestern University. I rode the bus to Indianapolis in 1943 to the Prohibition National Convention.

I broke my left little finger twice playing baseball. In each case, a hit ball impacted the end of my finger. I made my own splint from wooden matches. The break was confirmed later by x-ray.

I lived in a seven-room house on a double lot in Greenville, Illinois, until age nine. We had a large garden, raising several kinds of vegetables. We had no indoor plumbing or city water. I carried a bucket or two of drinking water daily from the outside faucet of Dr. Holtwick's home three doors to the east. To keep cool in the summer we slept on a sleeping porch which gave air circulation. We had one eight-inch non-oscillating electric fan with exposed brush terminals which, if touched, would shock you.

In 1938—39 we lived in a two-room apartment in Ann Arbor, MI. In Hillsdale from 1939—42 we lived in a seven room frame home before moving to a larger frame home at 306 N. West Street in 1942 to better accommodate the Scene-O-Felt work. In Ann Arbor I slept on a cot in a corner of the living room.

I first had a room of my own in Hillsdale at age 11, and when the building was expanded, my parents allowed me to have a "studio" adjacent to my room for my recording activities.

I could expect two orange sodas a year as refreshment, one on our annual trip to Ohio and one on our annual trip to Iowa, each to visit grandparents.

We had electric lights, primarily with 25 watt bulbs. I recall the first 75 watt bulb—a big blue "daylight" bulb—that my father purchased at the college. That bulb lasted from the mid-1930s into at least the late 1950s. It enabled my mother to do her work on dark days and at night.

2. Hillsdale

In 1937—38 Dad attended college full time at Northwestern University in Evanston, Illinois, completing a significant part of his doctoral course work in educational psychology. Mother remained teaching at Greenville where she started the Scene-O-Felt business. Scene-O-Felts were Bible-based stories illustrated with hand painted wool-felt backgrounds and figures. At one time this business grew to an equivalent of nine or ten fulltime workers.

We moved to Ann Arbor, Michigan, in the summer of 1938 when I was nine (I turned 10 in September). Dad had a teaching fellowship at University of Michigan where he taught educational psychology and completed his doctoral course work. He never did write the dissertation, but he was later given an honorary Doctorate from Hillsdale College.

They sent me to the University of Michigan elementary school. In September of '39 I was all set to start school again when Dad got a call from Hillsdale College. They had lost the head of their school of education and wanted to interview him. We went to Hillsdale to take a look around and talk to people. They made the decision, and we moved to Hillsdale the first week of September in 1939.

I had joined the church when we lived in Ann Arbor when I was nine years old. Then I transferred my membership to Hillsdale when we moved there, then to Coldwater when Ella and I moved there to start the radio station, and finally we moved our church membership to Spring Arbor when we retired.

I attended Hillsdale public schools, started at Hillsdale College in 1944 and graduated in 1947. By the time they awarded my diploma I was 19, but I had finished the course work at age 18.

I graduated from high school in a way—I have a diploma. World War II was on, and I had always been interested in aviation. Clear back when I was six years of age I was building airplanes out of balsa wood, tissue paper, and rubber band motors. Rather than buying the kits for 25 cents, I found I could buy the supplies and design my own that flew as well as the kits flew.

When I was in the ninth grade in Hillsdale, Mary Alice Smith was my English teacher. You had to take at least three years of English to graduate. She would stand up there in her flatfooted shoes and make her stupid statements. Her inadequate explanations of the material— and in the ninth grade it was literature—makes me shudder now. I had read everything she had in her library. My mother, with her degree in rhetoric, was far superior.

I went to Mr. Edwin Henry, the principal, and informed him that I would not be taking the required English course the following year. By this time I was the school's technical director. The only thing I didn't have a key to was the safe, and I knew how to pick that lock—I learned how to pick locks there.

He said, "You have to."

I said, "Mr. Henry, You don't understand. That woman doesn't know anything from anything, and I've read every book she's read and more. I've studied poetry, I've studied literature, and I CANNOT and I WILL NOT take 10th grade English."

"Well," he said, "we'll see what we can do."

I came back to school in the fall, and—lo and behold!—I was registered to take debate instead of English! I finished two years of debate and learned a lot. I was happy, he was happy, and she was happy to be rid of me.

One thing I did back then was to work with Pastor Richard DeMille at the old Free Methodist church to construct nearly exponential speaker horns from plywood (war time material shortages were a problem until about 1946). We installed them behind the existing slats in the stubby bell tower of the church. Each Sunday prior to service I would show up early and play 15 minutes or so of 78 RPM Christian music over the speaker system. We had no bell.

At the 1943 Prohibition Party presidential nominating convention in Indianapolis, IN, I took the opportunity to visit a radio supply and found a high powered amplifier which I purchased with my savings from mowing lawns. This served as the core amplifier for later servicing the Hillsdale College stadium for both high school and college games—for a fee, of course.

I constructed speaker horns from corrugated cardboard boxes I had salvaged, then painted them for weatherproofing and used them for several years until the war rationing of electronics was just a memory. During this period I accumulated a store of radio parts and experimented with carrier current service to the college campus, but I had no means to finance such a service.

My ambition was to join the military and learn to fly. I had read Lindbergh's book *We* several times. They were drafting people at age 18, and at that time you had to have two years of college in order to join the air force. I did not want to be in the infantry, I wanted to be a flyer, so Dad came up with an idea.

Dad said, "We're giving some multiple regression tests over here at the college. I'd like to have you take one to see how it turns out." So I took the test one Saturday, and in two or three weeks I received word that I had come out first in the group on this series of tests and was awarded a four-year scholarship.

Hillsdale College had eight fully paid academic scholarships each year. They went to the people who took the top eight positions on this examination. I was the only high school junior taking the exam and I happened to take the top position. That catapulted me into college early.

The scholarship meant my tuition costs were just $25 per semester, and I had considerable income from recording spot broadcasts for various commercial stations wanting coverage in that area. I had rehabilitated an old Presto recording lathe and updated the electronics to make this business possible.

So my strategy to get at least two years of college before being drafted into the military was to drop out of high school and go to college at age 15. I went and told the high school principal I was leaving high school to attend college and he said, "But you've got to have a high school diploma!"

In high school Jim Moench was a year behind me in school but my age or older, and Jim was also interested in technical stuff, so we shared the tech responsibilities at the high school. Three of us in the neighborhood usually walked the mile to school together, and I usually walked home for lunch and back to school, so I got four miles of walking in automatically. A group of us that were better students were in class together, and in those days the bright kids were put together, so that pretty much erased the age difference.

Before the year ended the superintendent must have come to understand how things were, so he struck a deal with me. He said, "If you'll come back next fall and take the state required, one semester of civics, then I will see that you get a diploma." Of course, he wanted me to stick around to solve all his technical difficulties—Jim and I pretty much had the run of the school. So I was awarded a general studies diploma at the end of that time.

All the way through college I always had an 8:00 a.m. college class. So I carried about 19 hours of college credits each semester and finished my degree in the summer of 1947. My major was physics, and I was just one credit short of a chemistry major, and six credits short of a math major, so it was a pretty husky credential.

In college the other kids were four years older than I was, so I was the odd person out, but I didn't mind at the time because I was busy with other things. For a couple years I took care of the public address and movie equipment at the high school, I was active in both band and orchestra playing French horn, and there was always something interesting to do.

When I was still in high school they also drafted me to play in the college symphony orchestra, and I continued to play with them in college. So I was all mixed up as far as age groups were concerned.

They gave me my college diploma the week after I turned 19, but in the meantime, about the middle of December of '46, my dad raised a question. He'd been insisting that I needed to take the necessary coursework to get a teaching certificate. I said, "I am not really planning to teach. I'm planning to mix dynamite or something like that in a chemistry lab at DuPont."

So anyway, I did take the necessary prerequisites for teaching, but I had a problem. The student teaching was a five-hour requirement which didn't fit into my schedule. But then Dad said he had a call from North Adams saying they had lost their science teacher and wanted to know if we could supply a student teacher to finish out the year.

In addition to carrying 19 hours of course work, I went to North Adams every afternoon and taught math and science at North Adams/Jerome schools for the winter and spring of 1947. Most of the high school juniors and seniors were older than I was.

I had 53 kids in an 8th grade science class—I had them literally sitting on the window sills there. Taking the time to teach those classes is probably what cost me getting a cum laude on my college grades. Since I was teaching biology as well as the science I knew about, I had to scramble to keep ahead of my biology kids. A couple of them turned out to be doctors, so I guess I didn't do too badly.

At the end of the school year at North Adams (I still had college summer classes to finish), out of the blue I got a contract from Greenville College inviting me to go there and teach physics and math for two years while the head of the department was finishing his PhD.

The superintendent at North Adams also wanted to keep me as a teacher there and give me charge of the junior high. He offered me more than twice as much salary as Greenville was willing to pay.

The car I drove back and forth to North Adams was a real early '47 Dodge. I borrowed $1,400 from my dad to buy that car. Of course, I didn't get paid for the student teaching. My brand new 1947 Dodge was a medium gray with red wheels. One of my friends in college was a Dodge dealer, so I was able to get that car right away, whereas most people after World War II had to wait up to 18 months for a new car.

Another unsolicited job offer came from Michigan State University. They sent me a contract for a teaching fellowship in chemistry. I took a look at that. I would be lecturing 200 freshman chemistry students while working on an MA in chemistry. However, housing was not available, and I was more interested in physics.

Then I got word of a vacancy at Pittsford, a Rural Agricultural School. The chemistry and physics teacher had moved on. At North Adams I would have had to teach biology again, and the pay was the same, so I went to Pittsford. When I arrived they said, "Oh, by the way, our biology teacher left—you'll also be teaching two sections of that."

As my life actually played out, after college graduation I taught the same courses I had taught as a student teacher at North Adams for another year, and I helped coach football. The following year, I went to Pittsford and taught for one year. I drove back and forth every day between Hillsdale and Pittsford. Gas was 19 cents a gallon, and my Dodge was paid for by then.

I would never casually advise youngsters to push their education ahead in the fashion as I followed unless, like me, they were in extenuating circumstances and faced the probability of draft into a service they didn't care to pursue.

Upon graduation from college I was still 1-A draft status and volunteered for the OCS program in the Navy, and I even knew the unit I was to be assigned to. Out of 15 applicants, I was the only one who didn't have an MA degree. But they lost my papers, and by the time they worked it through, the hostilities were winding down.

Later, working with a client in San Francisco, one man kept looking at me in a strange manner. He finally made a statement that revealed the question in his mind, and I responded by addressing him with his earlier military rank. He immediately recognized me from the 1951 interviews and said he always wondered why I never showed up in Korea!

I suspect the Lord may have had something to do with that intervention, for in that year I did the FCC and technical planning for KAIM-FM in Hawaii and the important Christian Broadcasting Association and Billy Graham Evangelistic Association ministries that developed from that station.

3. Radios

In 1949, I made the decision to quit teaching and go into radio, a subject I had been long interested in. As a child in Greenville my dad took me to see Howard Winters' ham radio station. I was intrigued.

I had a continuing interest in radio, and during the early war years I took my lawn mowing and odd job money and bought recording equipment and set up a recording studio in our house. When my parents built on to make room for the Scene-O-Felt business, they built a little sound-proof room off the back of my bedroom. I made quite a bit of money recording high school choirs and field recordings of things of interest to Hillsdale College, and on a freelance basis I made recordings for WOWO (Fort Wayne) and WKAR (East Lansing).

I got my commercial radio operator license from the FCC at age 14. I just studied up on all the books, played around with simple radio designs, and took the test up at the FCC offices in Detroit. You could get a driver's license at age 14 at that time, so I drove myself over to Detroit and took that test.

The FCC test was not easy, but it's a pass/fail type thing, and they ask a lot of totally off-the-wall technical questions. Fortunately, I had studied the books. There were circuits on that test you would never see in real life, and you had to know some maritime radio law as well as regular radio law. I had studied the books, and so I passed that four-hour test.

You had to draw diagrams. I remember feeling a bit disgusted when the test asked me to draw a working Loftin-White circuit that was outmoded in the '20s. They asked for just the three main circuits, but I covered a page with all five or six of the actual circuits. I watched the paper grader on the other side of the glass having to study my circuit drawing for quite a while. I was happy to be able to put him through that difficulty after the four hours they had just put me through.

I believe I was one of the youngest persons in the nation to hold the first class license. It had a five-year life and required at least three years of logged work involving transmitters for auto renewal. I was Member No. 2000 when the Society of Broadcast Engineers was organized, and I hold a life membership.

While teaching at North Adams, my interests shifted to radio because the war was over and radio was expanding rapidly. The coach at North Adams and I were chatting one day and he said his brother in Coldwater was interested in radio. So we organized a small group, pooled our finances, and filed an application to the FCC to establish WTVB-WANG Coldwater.

The application itself was only 25 or so pages plus supplemental exhibits regarding programing, financing, ownership details, etc., but it took two years to get the construction permit. Beyond that, I had to establish the radio frequency and broadcasting power, build the towers, and acquire the FCC and federal aviation air space clearances. All that plus clearing the local zoning requirements took all my spare time while teaching.

The permit came through in the winter of 1948—49, and when the frost came out of the ground in March, I spent Saturdays on site digging by hand the post holes that would support the transmission lines out to the towers. I finished the school year and then put full time into completing the station.

I won't go into detail on what all goes into building a radio station, but I will say I have climbed 75 feet and 100 feet up a radio tower for various reasons. My brother, Looey, was known to go as high as 400 feet. I don't recommend radio-tower-climbing as a career path.

I borrowed a hunk of money and put it into stock investments. The salary I got from the station was about half what I had been getting as a teacher—when there was enough money to go around after paying the employees first.

4. Charlene Ella Bronson (by Ella)

I met Harold when I first came to Michigan in 1945. I had planned on heading right to college the next fall, but I had two sisters working at the Munn Scene-O-Felt studio, and they invited me to come up right after high school graduation for a two-week vacation.

I stayed for two weeks, and Harold's mother put me to work in the office because they needed a secretary. They talked me into staying for the whole summer, and when fall came they were so busy that they talked me into staying the full year. I ended up staying two years. The second year was when Harold and I started dating.

After I had been up there in Hillsdale for two years I went to college in Greenville. It was a basic freshman course. I wanted Bible and some business stuff, because I had taken two years of business typing, shorthand, and accounting, but I couldn't get that my freshman year of college.

So after one year of college I went back to work at the studio for the summer. Harold and I dated for about 15 months. We went to church together and stopped at that Jonesville restaurant. Sunday afternoon walks in the Slayton Arboretum are an especially fond memory. There was an unfinished area back over the hills and we would walk and talk and find commonalities of interest and discuss differences of opinion and really get a complete picture of each other.

Harold says that when we found something we disagreed about, we would spend time in study and consideration to determine whether that would be an ultimate sticking point or not. He says the roughest conflict we had was three or four months after we were married and I tried to feed him oysters. He took one bite and said, "Are these oysters?"

I said, "Well, what makes you think so?" And he said, "Are these oysters?" And then a few hours later he got to thinking, *why should I let a little thing like an oyster mess up a perfectly wonderful marriage?* Of course, I have never tried to feed him oysters ever since.

However, one time at the DuPont Hotel in Washington, D.C. Harold saw Oysters Rockefeller on the menu. He said, "Here you go, Ella. I'm not having oysters, but this is your chance!" So I ordered them. The first one went down ok. The second went partway down, stuck, and ended up in my handkerchief. So Harold likes to say, "That was the last oyster she ever tried to eat—she was cured of them, and I didn't have to do the curing."

On a full moon we had another date we enjoyed. We would drive out to the Bear Lake overlook—that was a beautiful sight—and we'd mutter sweet nothings to each other. In the fall one of those roads down there toward Bear Lake was very pretty—there's a lot of wild territory in Hillsdale County.

We didn't go to the movies then, but we had prayer meetings and revival meetings, and sister What's-Her-Name would always take off shouting when the 8:10 steam train made the stop there on the tracks about 500 feet from the church. They had a stanchion for filling the steam locomotive with water—a couple thousand gallons—followed by a double toot on the whistle for all aboard.

Before the train got gone, the sound of that whistle would overpower sister What's-Her-Name—she couldn't out-shout the steam train and had to give up.

I was not a Christian until that first summer in Hillsdale when Verdon Dunckel, the pastor there, persuaded me to go up there to the altar and pray to receive Christ. Old sister Barbara was up there at the altar with me. After that I lived a life of faith.

I had never gone to a movie. Dorothy and I—neither one of us were making a Christian profession, and back then going to a movie was really considered a sin—but we wanted to see what a movie was like. There was a revival meeting at the church, and we secretly decided that after the service ended we would attend the movie and see what it was like to really sin. But of all things, my sister Dorothy went to the altar that night and was saved, so we never did get to the movie—I lost my chance!

I think the first moving picture I ever saw was the Billy Graham presentation of *Tora Tora Tora!* That was after Harold and I were married and we were out in Honolulu, Hawaii, working on that radio station.

When I was growing up my mother was a really good Christian, and while my dad was not a Christian, Mother was very faithful in having family prayer. And even though Dad was not a Christian, for a time he read the Bible after our evening meal, and then Mother led in family prayer.

Dad would participate with us even though he himself never did make a profession while my mother was living. I do remember when he came to church, because I would sit on his lap.

Then for some reason he quit going to church. I think there was somebody in the church—my uncle—every time they would have an altar call, this uncle would always go beg my dad to go to the altar, and that may have been why he stopped going to church, but after Mom died and he remarried, he did go to another church in town, the Christian Church, with this new wife.

I often wondered whether he ever became a Christian. He was a wonderful man, he was good, and when we were at home he would read the Bible for family prayer. He was a carpenter at the coal mine. He built our house—he was a good carpenter. My grandma lived next door and he built her house as well.

Oh yes! I was telling you about dating Harold. Well, he proposed to me after about 12 months of dating, but I made him wait three months because I wanted to be sure it was the Lord's will. I prayed about it, and God didn't give me a "no" answer!

It was on the porch of the Beehive where Dad asked for an answer and I said, "You're a day late!" I had given him three months, but he must have counted the actual days and there must have been a 31-day month in there. I've never doubted whether marrying Harold was the Lord's will.

In the Scene-O-Felt office I did the book keeping, accounting, took letters in shorthand, and typed. The office was right next to Harold's room, and from time to time I could see him, sort of. The door was shut. That was where he had his recording studio.

We girls lived about five houses down the street from the studio in a house we called the Beehive. The most we had there were about seven or eight ladies, and in the Beehive there were different jobs—cleaning, mowing the lawn, working in the garden, washing the dishes, cooking, and taking out the garbage. The ladies rotated between these jobs each week or month. My older sisters Edith, Virginia, Dorothy, and myself were there, plus three others including Cora Mae Jewell.

We were the last wedding in the old Free Methodist Church behind the post office in Hillsdale before the church was torn down. Louella Mae (Harold's mother) thought we were too young for marriage at 21 and 22 years of age, but after a while she got used to the idea. Our flower girl, Charlene Shepherd, forgot that Michigan was on Eastern time and got there late for the wedding. Verdon Dunckel preached our wedding, and Harold's father assisted.

After we were married on Dec 19, 1949, we lived in Hillsdale for six months in an apartment on West Street. Harold had put the Coldwater radio station on the air August 6, 1949, so he had his own company going at age 21, and I kept working at the studio, so Harold drove to Coldwater every day.

The summer of 1950 we moved to Coldwater, and after a short time I went to work at the radio station to do the accounting. I have been Harold's executive secretary ever since. Our first office was a combination bedroom and office. Both the bed and the long steel table were there. He would work on the maps and lay them out over the bed!

5. Consulting and the FCC

I established the Coldwater Radio
Engineering Consulting firm out of necessity late
in 1950. There was a glaring lack of competency
in what was called the radio engineering
community because the bulk of the people
working in that field were electrical engineers
whose studies ended with 60 cycles—they were
power engineers rather than *wave* engineers.

Wave engineers work with physics, the basic
stuff nature is made of. It is mathematically
based. I had been interested in radio waves since
I was eight years old. Howard Winters was a ham
radio operator whose home-built equipment
fascinated me. I followed that through all the
way to radio operation, and the FCC test I took at
age 14 was basically about the generation and
control of radio waves.

To build the Coldwater station, we hired
engineers because I was not qualified, but when I

saw the lousy work they did, I said, "This shall not be!" So I re-engineered the whole station and vastly improved the facility and went on from there to help other stations. Power, frequency, and coverage were the major issues that needed to be tweaked.

We held interest in that station until 1983, but I was putting the majority of my time into engineering consulting work from about 1953 on. I did not plan to manage the station at the beginning, but the man we hired never showed up, so I had to do it. We hired our first employees by the first of August. We had a licensed engineer, announcers, and a payroll of nine or ten at the outset. I hired a retired man from the cement mill to do the books.

Mom started out first by helping with preparing the logs. We had the program schedule, the commercial announcements, and the code from which advertisers were billed.

In 1959, we were the fourth radio station in the United States to put in the sophisticated IBM equipment to automate the logs. Ella went to

IBM school for two weeks, and we took care of our stations in Coldwater, Ypsilanti (WYSI), Hillsdale (WBSE), and Sturgis (WSTR). We also had FM facilities with a number of these stations, and Coldwater is the one I retained ownership of the longest.

I would say one important key to my success was paying attention to the footnotes. The footnotes sometimes contain a lot more facts than the text. Properly and honestly applied, they can take you a long way.

For example, the Mexican/United States agreement on broadcasting facilities that had been in effect for many, many years had established several absolutely clear channels for the Mexicans coast-to-coast. One was 1050 right in the middle of the band. There was no other station on that channel except a very restricted one in New York City that was permitted when they scrambled the channels in 1941. There were between 200 and 250 daytime-only stations on 1050 at that time. On another of the Mexican clear channels, I had a client (the famous author James Michener) who with five other guys purchased a small radio station near Philadelphia, and I told them, I'd like to see this thing amount to something. So we increased power to 5,000 watts.

As is typical with government papers, regulations concerning this station were not well written. I went to the language of the footnote, and there I discovered a valuable gap in the technicalities. If you were a distance more than 650 miles from the Mexican border, you could establish nighttime stations on that channel in the United States. So I filed an application for my clients based on the footnote facts, and I also filed a ruling to encapsulate proper wording in the treaty with Mexico.

So there are perhaps 1,000 stations operating at night because of this groundwork I did. This enraged the engineering staff at the FCC because they wouldn't admit to their mistakes, and it did not increase my popularity quotient there. The engineering department of the FCC had more foreign languages spoken than the ghettos of Washington, D. C. Many of the engineers there didn't even know what the United States Constitution is, but they sure knew how to object to the extra work load I may have caused them.

The first thing that set me apart from other engineers in my field was the ability to read and understand. Between reading my mom's books in rhetoric and my dad's books on educational psychology, I came to understand a great deal. As a boy I also read the entire *Encyclopedia Britannica*, and through this informal education I learned to think deeply and to choose the right word and use it accurately.

6. Coldwater Board of Public Utilities

I began serving on the Coldwater Board of Public Utilities (BPU) in 1960, was elected president of that board in 1967, and served in that capacity until 1995 when I retired and moved to the Spring Arbor neighborhood.

Probably my singular achievement was the time I went in there as president and I said, "You enjoy your cigars and your cigarettes, but you're killing me with your smoke. Either we don't have smoking in the board meetings, or you have my resignation." What happened? No more cigars, no more cigarettes.

What got me interested in serving in the first place was the attempted transfer of the electric system from the city to Consumers Energy. I knew Consumers' record of service was not good, and they had inadequate transmission lines into Branch County, both voltage-wise and capacity-wise. In fact, in the summer when load was heavy, they even had instances where the lines melted down and ignited the farmers' wheat fields.

The way I fought the proposal to sell out to Consumers Energy was to organize a small group that put together some money to buy newspaper ads and radio spots to point out why this was a bad idea. Our cutest ad was a big block of totally black ink with a note saying, "Coldwater's future if we sell out to Consumers Energy."

My opponents raged about that ad, saying it was improper advertising. We said, "Well, figure out your own ads as to why it makes sense."

They said, "Look at all the money we'll get if we sell out," and I said, "Yeah, and look at all the money you'll pay forever."

So I led the fight against the big political campaign to get Consumers in. When we won— their proposal was defeated by the voters—the board resigned and the mayor had to appoint a new board that included me.

The way we ran things made a lot of money for the city. We enabled the city to improve the electric system, the water system, and the waste water treatment system, all without going into general obligation bonds. We just used our profits to pay for things as needed, and we completely re-did the overhead wiring in the town to three-phase—brought it up into the 20th century.

We pumped the city drinking water from deep wells, and we located the sewage treatment plant on the west end of Coldwater. We discharged the treated effluent into the Coldwater River, maintaining the purest discharge water in the state of Michigan— actually in the six-state region.

The water we discharged into the river was cleaner than the water already there. This is at the headwaters of the St. Joseph River, so we had the highest requirements of any city. I have an award from the federal government recognizing that accomplishment.

We generated our own electricity—we had an older steam plant and a newer diesel plant, and very carefully determined what would be the best fit, and grew our resources that way.

I can't tell you today because it's too exhausting, but my story of the battle with the EPA and our victory was something else. Suffice it to say that science prevailed; political idiocy failed. To this day, Coldwater's Board of Public Utilities is the principal and largest member of the South Central Michigan power agency headquartered at Litchfield. This June, they will retire the steam plant after 19 years of outstanding service and replace it with stupidity—purchasing power from such places as South Dakota and Minnesota.

There was no pay for this job. It was civic responsibility. I figure that if you're receiving the benefits of being part of a town, then you should offer a little bit of payback if you can, and I had the administrative leadership and the technical knowledge they needed. And I could bring it forward non-Trump style. It wasn't "Look at me, look at me, look at me." Rather, it was, "Look at what the future is for Coldwater."

The entire board appointed by the mayor of people in agreement with these policies made it easier to get things done. We had honest discussion, good planning, and knowledgeable engineers who knew how to work things through and avoid the ever-present people who would buy their votes if they could.

7. About My Airplanes

After starting the consulting business, I found myself chartering flights to various customers as the most efficient travel strategy. My pilot flew a Cessna 180, a four-seat plane very popular with missionaries and bush pilots in remote areas. I rode in the pilot seat with him and worked out a deal where he would instruct me as we went from Coldwater to wherever I was working. This went on for a couple of years. I built up quite a bit of logged student time, and then spent specific time practicing maneuvers students are required to demonstrate for getting their license, and then I got my private pilot's license.

My first plane was a 1956 Cessna 172 that I bought slightly used in 1957. This was a tri-gear: a nose wheel and two main wheels; a single engine prop plane. It would cruise at about 125 mph. I bought this plane for $7,000 back in the day before liability insurance almost sank the aviation industry. Today, you can hardly buy an approved aviation radio for that price.

Then in 1958 I traded it for a 1957 Cessna 182 which is similar in design, only it has a significantly larger engine, a controllable pitch prop, more rugged construction, and it is faster. It cruised at about 150 mph and I typically flew at an altitude of 7,000 to 9,000 feet.

I had that until 1960 when I traded it for a Cessna 310, a five-seat twin engine. I was doing a lot of night flying, and actually it was Hugh White who owned an interest in the Cessna dealership in Ann Arbor—Twining—and he said he didn't want me flying around in a single engine plane.

So that was the big push, and I got a real good deal on it too—in the neighborhood of $40,000. With two engines, if one quit, you could still fly. It cruised at about 180 mph, but it was not pressurized, so I seldom flew at above 12,000 feet. I could go higher using oxygen masks for everybody on board, but I rarely did.

That plane lasted me until 1964 when I traded it for a Cessna 310 F, one of only six built for military personnel transportation. Its specifications were different from those built either before or after. It had a ruggedized landing gear, a lower landing speed, and a slightly higher top speed in excess of 200 mph. None of the 310s were pressurized. Of course, none of these planes had a bathroom, but this one did carry a "relief tube" which released into the airstream and caused a rainy day down below.

In 1975, I switched to the Cessna 340 pressurized plane with supercharged twin turbo props with 340 horse power for takeoff and 325 horse power for continuous operation. This was a six-seat plane and I could maintain sea-level pressure between 8,000 and 9,000 feet, and comfortable, safe breathing up to 18,000 feet. It also had supplemental oxygen available and could have gone up to 25,000 feet, but I never took it up that high.

Flying at between 12,000 and 17,000 feet, the range I normally operated at, put me above the general aviation traffic and comfortably below the commercial jets. After I did the RAM conversion on it, this plane had a cruising speed of 260 mph. I flew this plane until I sold it in 1993. It would have been a good investment to have held on to that plane—you would pay half–a-million dollars for that plane today—but I bought it for around $80,000 including the value of trading in the previous plane.

Whenever I needed a plane after that I rented one, and the last time I flew myself somewhere was around 1994. I still have my license, but Ella says she wouldn't fly with me if I were the sole pilot! Ella enjoyed flying, but she says, "I was always a little bit apprehensive and would always keep my eyes on the instruments in case Harold missed something."

An interesting incident occurred when I had a meeting to attend in Asheville, NC, with the Billy Graham broadcasting people, and I had just gotten the 340 aircraft back from its annual re-licensing. Ella was going down with me and it was a mixed day with towering cumulous clouds, breaks in between on this end, and basically an instrument approach into Asheville—no unusual thing. We took off from Coldwater and I was probably at 14,000 to 16,000 feet, and as we were climbing up through the clouds, my artificial horizon died, and my directional gyro died.

Those are two instruments that we rely upon quite generally, but you still have to demonstrate and be trained in the very basic instruments that General Doolittle pioneered back in the late 1920s when he first demonstrated instruments-only flight.

Those instruments are your turn-and-bank indicator and your airspeed indicator, commonly known as needle-ball-and-airspeed. When you qualify for instrument flight, you've got to demonstrate that you can indeed fly with the more sophisticated instruments covered up and can safely control the aircraft using needle-ball-and-airspeed.

I was interested in getting to Asheville and was disgusted because I'd just gotten the plane back from relicensing. I surmise that what happened is that some assistant mechanic had goofed up the vacuum supply to the gyros.

We went ahead and made the flight, and the instrument approach is based on radios, so we made that fine, and when I got back to Michigan I took it back to the shop and they fixed it. That was proof of the value of thorough training to be able to fly under adverse conditions and basic instrumentation.

By the way, have I told you the Bishop Cryderman story? That story involves the Cessna 310F landing three feet too low. The bishop had called me up because he was on a tight schedule, having committed to speak at the Oakdale Christian Academy Commencement in Kentucky, so he called to ask the favor of whisking him down there. He brought his wife, Dorothy, and I brought my wife, Ella, and we headed out.

On the return flight at about midnight approaching Coldwater, everything was normal and I came in for a straight-in landing on the runway. Suddenly I realized we had not touched down and our position was looking too low, but I was too close to the ground to add power to arrest the descent. The next thing I heard was scraping on the runway of the bottom of the aircraft.

I landed three feet too low because the landing gear had not extended. I had no warning that the landing gear was not down. I can't swear that I didn't forget to put the landing gear down, but it was a beautiful landing right straight down the runway. It damaged the aluminum on the bottom of the plane and one landing light. Of course, the props were shot because they hit the asphalt. Did about $6,000 worth of damage—you can do that much to your car these days hitting a deer.

When the plane stopped, the bishop knew what had happened, threw the door open, and shouted to the ladies, "Get out, get out!" The urgency was because we didn't know if there would be an explosion or something, but our wives were unaware that there was any problem until they stepped out of the plane, and it was just one step down.

I went back in the office, called the FAA, and they officially closed the runway until it could be cleared. The next day we jacked up the aircraft, dropped the gear down, put new props on it, and flew it to Pontiac where it was repaired.

8. Al Gore's Internet vs. Mine

Unlike Al Gore, I don't claim to be the inventor of the internet, but my broadband work was intended to make cable television generally available to the public on a reasonable financial basis. This in turn established the infrastructure that was instrumental in making the internet possible.

After my initial successes in radio, I began exploring possibilities in the new field of cable television. The first cable television loan that Harris Bank of Chicago ever made was to me in the amount of $240,000 to establish Coldwater Cablevision. Collateral for that loan included our home, our radio station, our consulting business—everything we had. My two investment partners were Floyd Eby and Eugene Dennis.

That money was used to buy land for the tower east of town, build the original 400' tower, purchase the equipment, build a facility to house the equipment and provide office space, and install coaxial cables to all the houses in town. The strategy was to capture the programming of other stations and provide those channels to our customers, and at that time there was no royalty fee to re-broadcast the signals we pulled in.

Broadband technology made cable television possible. Broadband means a frequency of operation from one end of the spectrum to the other. It can be carried over coaxial. Initially, it operated on vacuum tubes and that early signal was just entering the broadband spectrum. Solid state devices and transistors began replacing vacuum tubes around 1965, and this took advantage of a continually broader and broader spectrum of the available broadband.

Everything was looking good until the FCC decided to regulate this while we were still building the station in 1963. Some big Wall Street firms saw there was money to be made in this, and before I was able to acquire my permit, they prevailed upon the FCC to put a freeze on new cable systems. The big Wall Street guys saw the possibility of making this a worldwide communication monopoly and didn't want anybody messing up their act. Their motive was never to provide cable services at $4.95 a month as we intended to do.

If FCC permits for cable were frozen, it meant we could not continue, would lose our entire investment, and would be utterly bankrupt. In my protest against this, I was scheduled to appear at the FCC on a Thursday and Friday. At the end of those hearings they were very smug about it all and said, "Well, we'll have this decided in another year, or year-and-a-half."

"No you won't," I said, and I hopped into my plane and flew to Baltimore where I caught commercial flights to San Francisco and then to Oakland where I rented a bucket truck and headed into the mountains near Placerville where I needed to prove that they had no TV access. I worked in snow at the higher elevations and in rain at the lower elevations, but after a day of measuring the signals available to the general public, I had the data needed to make my case.

I returned the bucket truck, made the reverse trip to Baltimore where I picked up my plane and got back to Coldwater in time for a nap. Then I taught my usual Sunday school class in the morning, and then rested. I believe that if you honor God, he will honor you, so I always made sure to rest on the Sabbath.

The minute Sunday was over I got up at midnight because I had work to do on the raw material I had measured, and by five o'clock, the work was done. Ella was up as well, doing copy work, and then I went out to the airport and blasted off for Washington, D.C. in time to meet as scheduled with Gerald Ford, a Michigan Congressman I had interviewed on the air—a very decent and wholesome guy. I explained it all to him in his office in Washington, DC.

I placed the whole problem before this gracious gentleman, pointing out that I was not the only one impacted—that he had people with the same problem in the Thumb, Midland, Saginaw, Bay City—you name it. Then I said, "It just isn't American to deprive these folks of their right to the mass media."

The California data was strategic because it showed that the Michigan problem was not an isolated concern but rather typical of the entire United States. Everything we did was basically federal, not just state level, so it was applicable across the nation. Because Ford was from Michigan, I needed this California data to make clear the national dimensions of the issue. It was not just a Michigan pork barrel scenario.

At the end of our conversation, as I was going out the door, he grabbed the bowl of his ever-present pipe, pointed the stem of the mouthpiece at my chest and said, "Harold, you have my word, you will have your waiver of the FCC's action."

Gerald Ford's intervention saved my business, as did the actions a decade later of such entities as the 9th Circuit Court of Appeals in San Francisco, a very liberal court, which fortunately ruled against the giant corporations in favor of small operators. The various court rulings concerning the FCC over the years allowed us to succeed in the cable business. Coldwater Cablevision and two in California were the first to get permits from the FCC.

At one time we had about 11 cable permits and systems in such places as Coldwater, Quincy, Bronson, Brooklyn, and townships in the Clark Lake neck of the woods. I was instrumental in helping 50 or 60 other cable operators get established, and we also did a lot of early cellular telephone work along the west coast of Florida.

If the FCC rulings had gone the other way, cable television would have had much less diversity and much more control by major financial organizations. Our friend Al Gore who supposedly sponsored the internet worldwide— he didn't sponsor anything. He bought thousands of acres of jungle in the south, and if you wanted to break the law and put in a coal burning plant, you bought the rights from him to pollute. He was into the whole environmental thing for the money.

But that's not the core of the story. The core of the story is that we had three cable systems that represented the start of the internet, and of the three, I was the only one lobbying for it, and I took the battle right to the top and got it turned around in a week's time. I believe this was only possible because of the way I honored the Lord with my time by observing Sunday and teaching that class at church as usual. Honor God and he will honor you.

9. Pan American, Liberace, and Me

Two of the dominant airlines in the middle 1950s were Pan American World Airways and Trans World Airlines. Trans World flew the humpback Lockheed Constellation; Pan Am flew the double-decked Boeing Strata Cruiser.

Well, someplace in my memorabilia there's a copy of the local paper from out in Honolulu with me debarking at the old terminal on the south side of the field. The Royal Hawaiian band is playing, I'm standing on the top of the boarding steps waving to a crowd of 10,000 or so admiring fans, and Liberace is one step down in front of me.

What happened was that the weather was heavy, and flying from Detroit to Los Angeles on TWA we were running late, so I passed word up to the pilot that I had to make my connection to Honolulu—back then you could communicate with the flight crew, and soon enough word came back that arrangements were in place and I would make the connection.

As soon as we got into Los Angeles, they came on board and took me off and had a Jeep and drove me across LAX to the open door of the Pan American plane headed for Hawaii. I wasn't even seated yet when they slammed the door shut and started cranking. In those days the tourist section was in the front, and it was jammed with people.

I was sitting next to a gal going out to Hawaii to marry a serviceman coming back from Japan. All she could do was chatter, and I got tired of listening to that, looking at my watch every five minutes. So I grabbed my ditty bag and joined the line to the restroom that was backed half way up the aisle.

We were maybe a third or half way across the Pacific on this night flight. So, after determining that the stewardesses were either asleep or missing, I let myself back into the first class section of the plane which was entirely reserved by the flamboyant Liberace, the highest paid pianist of all time.

I slipped back into that restroom toward the tail, and in there they had prepared a table—all kinds of perfumes and ointments and other junk—as was befitting His Royal Highness.

Nobody was there!

I spent a good 45 minutes in there cleaning up, shaving, and living high on the hog. All of a sudden the plane turned end for end and up and down and all over the sky, and I clutched for grab bars and anything I could hang onto, and literally crawled out the door of the restroom, found a seat, and strapped myself in.

One stewardess had been preparing breakfast back at the tail kitchen. She came crawling up the aisle on all fours and buckled in next to me. For the next 45 minutes we bounced all over the sky in an unanticipated turbulence.

A cost-saving move by the military had reduced weather staffing, and we had hit a previously unidentified developing storm—as when a hurricane begins winding up tighter and tighter, and we flew right smack into the eye of it. Poor Liberace, sicker than a horse, was lying in his Pullman-style sleeping berth, and he kept buzzing for new blankets and having them pass things into him—he must have been a stinking mess.

When it all calmed down, the navigator came back and joined us—Liberace wasn't concerned about who was in all the first class seats, he was too busy with personal maintenance. He was going out to Hawaii for his candle-light concert.

The navigator settled in next to me and said he had been by himself on the flight deck—the pilots had been downstairs at the bar. And when we landed at Rogers Field, there were 10,000 screaming women out there who wanted to see Liberace.

Since I was where I was, I couldn't resist just following Liberace out of the plane. He didn't know or care who I was. So he stepped out of the plane with me behind him. I was a step higher and a bit taller than he, so I waved to my adoring audience, descended behind him to the tarmac, and commenced my business.

10. Family Matters (by Ella)

Harold and I have three children: Harold Derwin, Michael Douglas, and Marquita Renée. And my first name is actually Charlene. Don't ask me why we all go by our middle names—that is just the way it is in our family. I was named after my brother and my two grandparents—Charlene after my brother Charles, Ella after my mother's mother, and Elizabeth after my father's mother.

Derwin was born two years after we were married, and he was not a surprise. He was very much planned. In fact, all three of our children were very much planned, even though Derwin and Doug were very close together. And then, after all the boy genes were out of circulation, I was bound and determined to have a little girl. Dad kept telling me it was going to be a boy because he didn't want me to be disappointed, but I kept saying, "No, I know it's going to be a little girl."

Our house at that time was on Edison Court in Coldwater, and our office was just the den to the left of the front door with the kitchen behind it, and initially we had just one employee. When we added a second employee, we decided to build an office suite on the south end of the house in back of the garage. We could go directly from the kitchen into the office, so we probably had an easier time than many people do with managing work and family. Harold grew up with his mother's Scene-O-Felt business right there in the home and his father's office just across the street on the Hillsdale College campus, and we had pretty much that same setup in Coldwater.

While I was working I had a very dear friend, Grace Miller, who came into our home and helped with cooking and cleaning and taking care of the children. All of the kids loved her and she loved them. She was a dear, dear friend. If our children turned out well enough, it was with the Lord's help and the Christian training they got in the home. We were always at church Sunday morning, evening, and midweek, and the kids went to Christian Youth Crusaders (CYC) camp every summer.

The bedtime ritual involved family prayer together, and we would most always read a story. We had books they could pick stories from—*Uncle Wiggly* was a favorite. I would always tuck them in, give them a good night kiss, and then close the door—but not Renée's, because she would always cry if I closed her door all the way.

We always had a family trip planned. I made sure that we went on a summer vacation. Sometimes it was at our church family camp, or to the Angola Indiana State Park, and several times we went out west—to Yellowstone National Park, Glacier National Park, California Redwoods—sometimes we flew out west once we had an airplane. We visited the Canadian Maritime Provinces, Mammoth Cave in Kentucky, and the Bronson reunion trips every other summer. I am the youngest of the eight Bronson children, and every other summer throughout our lives we got together for reunions that lasted several days.

As much as possible, when Dad was home, we had meals together every day. We didn't eat on the run, and we would have family devotions. At first it was in the evenings that we read the Bible together—Dad read *Living Letters* when that new paraphrase started coming out, and we would kneel around the sofa for prayer. After Renée was five years old or so and Dad was frequently gone in the evenings to the various board meetings, then the family devotions were in the morning around the breakfast table.

Once Harold got on all those boards, he was gone an awful lot in the evenings. And he was gone a lot once he starting helping Dr. Bell with his new station WCHB in the Detroit area, or else he was involved in WYNC in Ypsilanti, but before all that it was WSTR in Sturgis, which followed not too far behind Coldwater's WTVB-WANG.

I stayed many times at home with just the three children because he was gone so much, but those airplanes of his made it possible for him to be home—I was very grateful for the planes, but even then he was often away for a week at a time if he had a proof of performance commitment at a new radio station. When he arrived back home he would "buzz" (fly low) over the house, and the kids were always excited to hear the plane swoop by, notifying us to pick him up at the airport.

After Harold started KAIM in Hawaii, he went out there sometimes two or three times a year when they first started, and at least once a year thereafter. I made 27 of the trips to Hawaii—about half of them—and we usually stayed for a couple of weeks. I set up the books for the station and worked the whole time I was out there, doing the accounting. After I had the books set up, I would go and help with anything needed to get the accounting straightened out. I didn't do much swimming out there in Hawaii.

The last few trips to Hawaii were more just vacation time, and when Harold was working I had time to crochet, and we went out for many, many delicious meals. I loved the food—the

Chinese food—and a few times Renée went with us. That was always a very enjoyable time.

I also went along quite often when he went out west on work projects. And sometimes he'd take Derwin or Doug on business trips. When they were older, they were needed to help measure the strength of the radio waves—proof of performance required hundreds of measurements in all directions to make sure the signal was contained where it should be.

In about 1971 when Renée was in junior high school, we built a new office building and airplane hangar out at the airport. Renée could either walk home from school or take the bus out to the office. She started doing office work for us in junior high, doing things like alphabetizing correspondence for me to file. We had a giant machine called a Copytron—you had to feed in one sheet at a time and it took about a minute to make one copy. Imagine how long it took to make a copy of some big filing, then three-hole punch and put it in a binding.

I enjoyed it all, but my favorite part of the job was bookkeeping—recording all the business costs, setting up all the different accounts, and keeping track of all the assets and liabilities, income and expenses. I pretty much did all that by myself. I also did our church books and radio station books.

We had our business, and we had our private life. Sometimes we would work all night to get reports out that had to be filed with the FCC at a certain time, and in the morning Dad would fly them directly to Washington, D.C. to meet the deadline. It seemed like there was always a crisis, because back in the early days of radio, there would be a list of cities with filing deadlines, and it seems like we were always hustling to meet deadlines.

11. Bell Broadcasting / Motown

I have been privileged over my career to be a part of a number of "firsts." Bell Broadcasting was one such first because it is the first African American-owned radio broadcast station established in the United States from the ground up through an application to the FCC. Frankly, there were a lot of rednecks in the FCC, and the African American applications never got acted on.

I was contacted by Dr. Haley Bell, the first licensed black dentist in Michigan. He had graduated from Meharry Medical College in Tennessee and then moved to Michigan in the early 1920s. Dr. Bell was qualified for a dental license, but back then Michigan would not license people of color, so he worked at Ford Motor Company until he was able to prevail against the state of Michigan, and when his license came through at mid-week, he never returned to Ford for his final paycheck.

He established his office in the Polish neighborhood of Hamtramck surrounding a GM plant, and the practice was chiefly Polish customers. Later on his two daughters, Iris and Doris, went to school in the south and married African American dentists who joined him in practice there in Hamtramck.

Dr. Bell was concerned also in many civic affairs and assisted in the establishment of a life insurance company to insure black people. He participated in organizing a cemetery association where black people could be buried, and indeed, until recently there was always one of his descendants on the board of that association.

He felt the need of media. There was a black newspaper published there, but no electronic media, so in November of 1952 we met on a cold, rainy day at the Flag Stop train platform serving Eloise Mental Hospital out at Inkster. It was just a canopy-like bus stop where we agreed to move forward. He employed me to do the engineering to prepare the application for a broadcast station. The previous new application established in Detroit had been in 1928.

You have to file an application for a construction permit with the FCC detailing all the technical specifications, precise location of the transmitting plant, protection of other broadcast facilities against interference, details of the ownership, who would operate it, and justify it on the basis of the "public interest, convenience, and necessity." They limited the number of commercials per hour and wanted to know the general type of programming.

Rather than applying for Detroit itself where Canadians had already taken most of the broadcast frequencies, we decided to apply at Inkster, heavily populated by African Americans.

Dr. Bell wanted to give an opportunity for black artists to perform music. In fact, later on Barry Gordy developed Motor City Records out of this. Our new station provided opportunities for African Americans to report news of the black community as well as general news—in other words, to integrate the life of the African American into the American citizenship dream.

The FCC was reluctant—not in writing, but on the part of the staff—because these were black people applying for this, but we pushed and prevailed. A week before they granted the application, I received a call from a white owner of a station programming to blacks in Cleveland, Ohio, offering me $25,000 to sabotage the application. I immediately flew to Washington and got with the attorney. We made the appropriate contacts with the FCC and within a week I came back with the permit.

From the time I first met with Dr. Bell until we received the permit was seven or eight months. You see, what was happening was that predominantly Jewish interests saw a developing market among the African Americans and wanted to control the media playing to them and keep the blacks down. They wanted to put the money in their own pockets. This was a major American city that would have a black-owned station.

The station began as a 500-watt daytime-only broadcast serving a 25-mile radius. Today, it is a 25,000-watt full time clear-channel station at 1200 on the dial. There is a mural in the basement of the Wright Museum in Detroit depicting faces and figures of the growth of African broadcasting enterprise in Detroit.

That $50,000 mural was designed and paid for by Bell Broadcasting to appear on the museum cafeteria wall, but now it is relegated to the basement. It depicts Dr. Bell and the many other stars who came up through the Bell Broadcasting Company.

From 1953 until Dr. Bell died of a heart attack, I worked for them continually advising on such things as building the tower, facility operation development, management questions, developing the whole business operation, and all the electronic components.

After Dr. Bell passed away, his wife, Mary L. Bell, served as CEO of BBC until she died at age 95. I was her close advisor, and during that period we developed the trust structure to conserve the estate after her passing. She died in the early 1990s, and the entire business was sold in 1995 to a fledgling entity in Baltimore, MD. This black-owned entity is now Radio 1, arguably the largest African American-owned broadcast operation in the United States, and the Bell establishment was their key station.

The Supremes and all the great Motown artists are greatly indebted to Dr. Bell—who is greatly indebted to me.

Mrs. Bell was smart. She knew that her wealth made her an attractive target, so she set up the trust to preserve the funds. Since that time I've been a trustee of the Mary L. Bell Trust. That work entails supervising the investments of quite a few million dollars. I use the wealth management department of Comerica Bank at the present time.

A trust first of all protects the principal. Secondly, it states the purpose for which it is held. Third, it states how funds will be distributed. Finally, it tells when the trust will be terminated (and therefore liquidated).

The rate of distribution that the attorneys strongly advised was higher prior to the 2008 financial debacle in this country. Back then, they advised distributing 4.5 percent of the principal per year, but now it is less than that because the recession impacted the amount of the remaining corpus of funds, so I have reduced the payout to conserve funds at least until the beneficiaries qualify for Social Security.

I had rather wide discretion as to special needs distributions, but I also tried to temper wisdom with judgment and know where there is abuse that could be involved in the requests.

Another trust I have managed is one that my dad set up for my brother and myself, but it ended up being used largely for his second wife, Nettie. I was the trustee of it, and it was not huge.

My father had twin sisters, and the twins had their teachers' retirement, which was quite good, and I also managed their little stash of money. They had their small bank accounts intended for covering funeral expenses. I have only about $1,100 left of those funds, and that is about what it will cost to put in Alice's gravestone. She is currently in an unmarked grave in Hillsdale by my grandparents.

12. Retirement?

Retirement for me was a gradual process of selling off the various businesses I had established over the years. It became more or less official when I sold my consulting firm to Wayne Reese, my very reliable employee and partner who started working for me as a junior in high school. Selling my last airplane was easily the most difficult thing I have ever done. No pilot ever wants to give up his wings.

With decreasing responsibilities in the world of broadcasting, I was able to assume increasing responsibilities as a trustee of the various ministries I have been privileged to serve. Ella and I moved to Spring Arbor in 1995 for the convenience of being closer to our children and grandchildren, it provided a shorter commute to commercial airports for the rather extensive traveling we did in retirement, and it put me at the hub of the Southern Michigan Conference of the Free Methodist Church. One thing I did in retirement was to put in time as a volunteer in that office.

I am in no condition now to recall my vast exploits as a church delegate to annual and general conferences over the decades—at one time I could have filled a very thick book with that—but to give you a taste of the sort of things that went on, I'll turn the microphone over to retired Southern Michigan Conference Superintendent William Cryderman whose father—the bishop—was my passenger that day I landed the plane three feet too low—with the landing gear still up.

"A tree is best measured when it is down"
—Robert Wilson

A stately figure of intelligence, influence, and unwavering commitment to Jesus comes to mind as I think of Hal Munn. When first visiting the Coldwater church as Conference Superintendent, Sharon and I were invited to the Munn home for dinner. There we enjoyed good fellowship, probing questions as to my goals for the conference, and a pledge of prayer and support as we began our new ministry.

This was followed up during the next few weeks, which then expanded into an offer to come along side of me as my "staff executive" as he called it. I immediately accepted gratefully, although wondering, "How will we ever pay for this?" I needn't have worried, for not only did he serve "gratis," but he faithfully showed up daily to attend to anything I needed.

His experience as Conference Secretary of course prepared him well. I could sit spellbound as he would launch into detailed history and background of experiences that led to decisions by the conference. When discussing particular churches, he likewise had an almost total grasp of the unique personalities of the conference churches. This often made me look wise beyond my years, thanks to Hal.

When communicating with conference churches, there were times when I was called to communicate difficult directives to a particular board or pastor. I would always give these letters to Hal to see if I said what was *intended. His response often was, "You have done a pretty good job if you want people to like you, but they won't have a clue as to what you are wanting!" He then would edit my letter, with the result that the reader would now know beyond a doubt what was intended.*

I should also say, occasionally Hal would originate a letter and run it by me to approve. So it was fun to say, "Hal, if we send that letter out, we will have a riot on our hands! Let me edit your letter." He would grin and approve my editing.

This did not infer a lack of kindness on his part. He was an astute businessman on a mission to make the conference churches the best in the denomination. His courage was always appreciated by the entire conference.

I could speak of his humor, of his vast knowledge on almost any subject, of our brainstorming sessions exploring various possibilities. And if I had a problem with my shortwave radio, he could always give me the electronic principle involved and I would nod and head for home to read my electronics dictionary.

I close with this. Hal was a pilot. He took his own plane on many professional trips around the country. But my mind goes to a trip not yet taken, but carefully planned. This Wesley hymn describes it:

I then rode on the sky, freely justified I
Nor did envy Elijah his seat.
My glad soul mounted higher
In a chariot of fire
And the moon, it was under my feet.

What a trip!

—*William Cryderman*

13. Spring Arbor University

My father was one of three finalists for Superintendent of Public Instruction of the State of Michigan when he was called to "rescue" Hillsdale College in their emergency. He was one of the planning committee of three that initiated the hugely successful Hillsdale College American Heritage and Independence program.

Dad always anticipated he would return to one of our Free Methodist schools or go to some Christian college—even though Hillsdale would have claimed to be a Christian college at that time. Dad turned down a job at Bob Jones University (thankfully so), and I later found a copy of the letter he wrote. He turned it down because he felt there could be the wrong spiritual emphasis as far as his son (me) was concerned.

Incidentally, I will say this: We lost so much territory in the evangelical Christian church between 1925 and 1940 because they were attacking the idea that knowledge and study of science was anti-Christian and damning the people who dared to break out of the limits to explore in these areas. I have informally called it the know-nothing era that set back the Church by thousands of people.

Anyway, Dad also turned down the presidency of Adrian College, a liberal Methodist school. And he turned down the vice presidency of Greenville College where he'd previously been dean, registrar, and head of the education department. He had two reasons for this decision. He would have been required to report to a boss who was a former student of his and in whom he did not have a lot of confidence. Then too, the President, Dr. Long, had followed Dr. Marston to the presidency, and he was insisting that my dad, in addition to carrying a full teaching load, complete his PhD within a limited time period. All that combined with a dramatic decrease in salary ruled out that decision.

When we went to Hillsdale, the Free Methodist Church there was set to close. The pastor's salary was barely $1,000 a year. The assumption was that we would have gone to College Baptist Church—it was a Baptist college. But we looked around and found this little unpainted, 28' x 40' Free Methodist Church behind the Post Office. We got involved there—and you know the rest of that story.

A butcher in Hillsdale, Elmer Pearson, for whatever reason, took an interest in me. When I was out at Wheaton College for a summer session, Elmer contacted me. He was interested in buying a radio station—WDGY—in Minneapolis, MN. He called me up at Wheaton and asked me to take a day or two off of school and run up there on the Northwestern 400, a train that really flew. I went up there, inspected the premises, and gave him my report—the place was all rundown and would have to be re-equipped. They were asking $400,000 for the station, and in my estimation it would have taken another $400,000 to bring it up to par. He decided not to buy the thing.

Elmer owned an *Er Coupe*, a model of plane no longer made. It was unique with single control, rudder, ailerons, everything all hooked together—with a 65 horse power engine.

Elmer learned how to fly that thing—it wasn't difficult—and invited me to go flying with him one day. It wasn't long after that—probably after I had the Coldwater radio station—that Elmer nominated me to the Spring Arbor College board of trustees. It was before Spring Arbor hired David McKenna to replace President Roderick J. Smith. Those were tough, tough days, and I joined the board back then.

At Hillsdale College there were problems that Dad would bring home and write up and verbalize about. I knew to keep my mouth shut from what I heard, but I got a liberal education in college administration. One of my early strengths was having observed a lot of academic problems and their resolutions.

I also corrected a lot of papers. I enjoyed it because I learned a lot of material that I never would have come across just sitting in class. I had an answer key, but to relate the answers to the questions was also educational. That was a kind of soaking-in experience. When you grade the same test multiple times, you learn the material. There were classes I never took officially that I probably learned more about than the actual students in the class.

At the beginning of my work at Spring Arbor, I was not in the inner circle. Hugh White, who literally saved the school from bankruptcy in the mid-1930s, he *was* the inner circle. He loved the school and as late as the last hour of his life was still signing papers for them—gifts and so on.

I never learned the totality of the problem with President Smith, but there was some internal problem. Back then when you had a tiny faculty and fewer than 100 students, you had plenty of room for gossip, misrepresentation, and unhappiness.

Smith was a B-24 pilot during the war, so he *had* to know how to be nice. That plane was built up at Willow Run, and if you didn't fly it correctly it would slam you right into the ground. I think he was involved in bombing oil fields in Ploesti, Romania. That explains his personality—he was a detail guy. He didn't know how to raise money, handle internal conflicts, and be diplomatic with potential donors. He just didn't have the personality for a president although he was a very nice guy. So he was better suited to public education, and he went on to be a school superintendent and later served a term as a college board member.

I was on the old Southern Michigan Conference campground at Oak Park one summer afternoon back in the days when conference was held in July. Someone came around from the school and whispered the word that David McKenna was the new president—he had earlier been brought in as academic dean.

McKenna served for several years, and I was at a conference gathering at the Jackson church when he was the speaker. At the close of his message he said, "It's been very nice serving here, and I have just accepted a position as president of Seattle Pacific University." We were about as crestfallen as you can imagine. That's when we drafted Woody Voller as the new president.

We had a trustee at Spring Arbor who insisted on rewriting of the bylaws to put in term limits. It has not worked here, and they copied it at Asbury, and they've had to waive it there. I see no good from it outside of giving them a means to get rid of dead heads. But there is a way to do that without term limits—the same way corporations do.

When my terms as a trustee at Spring Arbor expired, I was called back at least three times— they waived the rules to bring me back on the board. Each case of them bringing me back involved chairing or advising on search committees for the next president.

At times this can be tricky business. I'll give you one example. As soon as we employed

President Chuck Webb, I gave him a call—I had done some plain and fancy maneuvering to get him approved, because the expectation was that the president would need to be a Free Methodist.

So I did my due diligence and anticipated a challenge. I went to Bishop David Kendall and said, "Bishop, you have a person who years ago was not only a member of the staff at Spring Arbor, but also was ordained in the Wisconsin North Illinois Conference. When he left Spring Arbor College for another position, whoever was bishop and superintendent back then located him at some little point out in Wisconsin."

Then I said, "We want to hire this man as president of the college. I want the conference to reactivate his membership."

His mustache wiggled a bit, he allowed as how it might be done, and I learned a day or two later that it had been done. So we went ahead and appointed Webb. The first time Webb was introduced to the faculty as president, a faculty member (who shall remain anonymous) appeared to be terrifically angry as he said,

"What do you mean by bringing in a non-Free Methodist?"

"I said, "Please check your *Yearbook*!" He gulped, and that's the last I ever heard on that issue.

The work of a trustee is to serve the best interests of the institution with no thought of gaining popularity or recognition. In the above instance, my work was not appreciated. In the instance I am about to relate, my work goes unrecognized—which is no concern of mine, but it does make for an interesting illustration.

What happened is this: I was aware of the need to expand Spring Arbor's athletic facilities, and then I discovered a newly fabricated Butler Building in storage that had been designed as an airplane hangar. In due course that building was purchased, delivered, and assembled under a new identity as the Dunckel Gym on Spring Arbor's campus. A trustee makes such things happen with all the resources and talent at his disposal. It is not work for the faint of heart.

I would say one major accomplishment in my tenure at Spring Arbor was probably in getting them to look beyond the village limit sign and realize they are a regional university. That has not been totally realized yet, but we had a consultant come in years ago from Wheaton, back when we had an enrollment of only five or six hundred, who said, "You do not realize that you're sitting on the best kept secret in the Midwest in terms of Christian higher education. What you do with it is your responsibility."

I started Spring Arbor's radio station in the 1960s because I felt they needed better visibility in the world outside. It reached its height of perfection in the 1990s under the leadership of Carl Jacobson. My investment to build that station involved giving equipment, engineering services, and useful legal information. Over the years we've invested probably three to four million dollars into that station.

All that aside, my best memories are of the deep and meaningful relationships that have developed over the decades. I think this sentiment is best reflected in a letter my daughter, Renée, recently received to share with Ella and me when I was in no condition to get out of bed. My highly respected colleague David McKenna wrote:

> *Dear Renée:*
>
> *Jan and I have had such a warm bond of love with your folks for so many years, we feel as if we are part of the family. We pray for Hal and Ella by name every day and want them to know of our sustaining love during these critical days.*
>
> *Even before the diagnosis, Hal had written about his retirement from the ATS Board. Because he responded affirmatively to my request for consideration as a member of the Board of Trustees when I went to ATS in 1982 (just as he had in 1960 when we went to SAC), I asked if a plaque could be placed in the lobby of the chapel with the designation, 'Exemplar of practical holiness.' I could go and on with evidence confirming that tribute. I want him and Ella to know of our esteem as represented by this tribute.*
>
> *Jan and Ella connected with a rare sisterly love. It is not diminished by time*

or age. Please let her know how much Jan loves her and talks about their relationship.

With His joy and our love,
Dave and Jan McKenna
March 14, 2016

14. Asbury Theological Seminary

When my dad was dean at Greenville College he served under President Marston, and it was Marston who brought in the 16-millimeter films to campus that Bird had shot when he was in Little America, Antarctica, down there on the Ross Ice Shelf. When I went to Antarctica a few years ago with my son-in-law, it was the Shackleton route; Bird went in from the New Zealand side of the planet.

Once he became bishop, Marston traveled largely by bus, and every time he got stuck in Michigan, he'd call my dad and say, "Do you suppose Junior could drive me back to Winona Lake, Indiana?" So my dad volunteered my chauffeur services many times over.

On those long drives together Bishop Marston would think out loud about the various challenges he faced, and training clergy was a major concern. He pontificated about whether to locate a seminary in Indianapolis, or whether to establish a seminary program in Greenville where he lived. Or, he reasoned, possibly Spring Arbor was the right location because of its central location and available real estate and the way such a program might help overcome the basic weakness of the school. Then too, he considered the value of such a program at Roberts Wesleyan due to its historicity in the Free Methodist denomination.

But he couldn't put together a library in any of those locations as easily or as well as the one which Asbury Seminary already had. Putting together a faculty would also be a challenge, and at that time eight of the Asbury faculty were Free Methodists. Then too, the good bishop was having problems putting together the church's own finances, and he never did reach the point of being able to recommend that our denomination establish its own seminary.

So Marston forged an agreement with Asbury that insured a certain number of Free Methodists on the board (I have actually been replaced by two Free Methodists—Debra McKenna Blews, secretary of the ATS board, and David Goodnight, prominent Seattle attorney).

A significant problem in those days was what I call the know-nothing mentality in significant portions of the church. At the root of it all was the blustering superintendent of the Pittsburg Conference with the gold watch chain across the belly of his ample vest. After Spring Arbor President Dr. Lowell made a very sensible and thoroughly prepared presentation on four recommended tracks toward ordination, I can remember to this day that the big fat superintendent from Pittsburg stood with his right hand pointed to heaven and intoned, "There are men who are called of God, and there are men who go to college."

I was not a delegate, but I was down in the press pit beside the platform. I don't think I spoke very loudly, but Bishop Fairbairn was on my side of the room and must have overheard what I said to one of my colleagues—that any rational person would support Lowell over the

Pittsburg fellow. Bishop Fairbairn came over and roundly excoriated me. I think I left the delegation at that particular point in time.

At that same session they removed the footnote from the *Discipline* which forbade the wedding band. That was never in the *Discipline*, just in a footnote, and immediately thereafter they adjourned the session. As they poured out the front door of the church, the son of the Pittsburg Superintendent stood up on the steps of the church and said, "Now we have lost it all!"

Well, this is part of the know-nothing era of opposing education. They were trying to take us back to the idea of people who had been converted in the back woods at a revival meeting and feeling called to being an exhorter—but what a difference between an exhorter and a thoroughly trained preacher or pastor.

We lost New Orleans Seminary in Wisconsin (see Marston's *From Age to Age a Living Witness* for details) and a couple others, and the whole picture was that the church was going to hell in a textbook. We are only now perhaps beginning to recover, and we don't necessarily know how best to achieve a balance between academic rigor and spiritual devotion.

Well anyway, those are some of the life experiences that may have equipped me to serve as a seminary board member, but it was not until 1983 that David McKenna, who had meanwhile become Asbury Seminary's president, invited me to go there and speak about communications and academia at some major gathering of the trustees. Howard Winters was retiring from that board, and he was one of the Free Methodist representatives, so he kind of nominated me for that spot.

At the time I joined the board we were in decent financial condition, and very shortly thereafter McKenna brought in a big hunk of Beeson money—a bequest of something like $41 million from a man who had never set foot on campus. His money funded several new buildings and programs, and through McKenna's careful stewardship, proper investment, and subsequent distributions, the $41 million grew into the range of $85 to $90 million. Today, Asbury has an endowment in the neighborhood of $150 million, and they are in the middle of a campaign to raise an additional $100 million for the 100th anniversary in 2023—the goal being to scholarship people graduating for the ministry rather than graduating in debt.

I count the current provost of Asbury Seminary as a great leader in the church today overcoming the know-nothing mentality. He compliments President Tennant's ministry and the establishment of Asbury as a leader in the Wesleyan movement in the world.

We have instructors now working on six continents, and agreements with major national institutions of Wesleyan origin, strengthening them, helping them, and giving them academic status. And we have established a tremendous library that's not just a library for its own self, but addressing an issue of world service.

The seminary has prospered tremendously. We now have a campus in Orlando, Florida, to service the Hispanic clientele, and we've just opened a new campus in Memphis, Tennessee, for the core of the United Methodist Church that is faithful to the Word, and that will carry the battle forward in opposition to the absurd notions of Christian gay marriage and ordination of homosexual clergy. The pro-gay contingents from the West Coast and New England will rage against us, but we pray that a few outstanding and large Methodist churches like the 30,000-member church north of Houston who are faithful to the Word may prevail.

One exciting thing at Asbury was when we finished building number 12 and completed the 160 beautiful new town houses at the main campus and tore down the last of the house trailers where people had lived in near poverty while going through seminary.

It's very rewarding to see all the provisions now in place. You have a dozen different nationalities with people from all over the world who attend, get doctorates, and go back home to establish reputable training programs for men and women in their home countries—establishing the Church as the Church should be.

Bishop Sundo Kim of South Korea, a trustee at ATS, and his wife donated a lovely building almost in the heart of the townhouse group on campus that gives a gathering place for families, and it dramatically improves the whole picture of togetherness, family, and cooperative worship, because they have a couple dozen denominations there, but people are not divided by that. Rather, they are working in common purpose to enhance their understanding of the truth of the gospel as taught by John Wesley as opposed to John Calvin and his five mistakes.

What I brought to the Asbury board was mature consideration of issues on which there were two very logical positions possible. Frequently at the meetings I would be among the last to speak because there were scholars around that table with enough degrees to tattoo your arm. I would listen to their arguments and presentations, and then toward the end I would signal the chair and say, "Could I speak a word?"

I was never denied that request, so I was able to move ahead and say, "It appears to me that there's *this, this*, and *this*, but a logical course of action would be if we would concentrate on doing *this*." I didn't win every time, but I didn't have to. I didn't always have to carry the full support of everybody to feel I had made an important contribution. If this little book comes to publication of any sort, I certainly want Tim Tennent to get a copy.

Note: The above conversation took place the day after Hal received a plaque with the words inscribed below and the accompanying letter from Asbury:

In recognition of

E. Harold Munn, Jr.

"Exemplar of Practical Holiness"

Board of Trustees

1983-2015

Asbury Theological Seminary

February 29, 2016

Dear Hal,

Greetings from Asbury Theological
Seminary.

    As David McKenna has
recommended, we are placing a plaque in
your honor in the lobby of McKenna
Chapel. A copy of the plaque is enclosed.
The brief words on it do not do justice to
the many, many years of service you have
given to the Seminary as a member of our
Board of Trustees. When David invited
you onto our Board in 1983, he likely had
no idea your tenure would last more than
30 years.

    During this time, which has spanned
the terms of five presidents of the
Seminary, we have been the recipients of
your wisdom, good common sense, and
your love for God and for the Free
Methodist Church. As the plaque says so
well, you are truly an "exemplar of
practical holiness." Thank you for being a
part of our Board during both turbulent
and triumphant times.

    We have learned of your illness with
great dismay. We are praying for you and
Ella as you meet this new challenge. May

*God's peace and comfort be yours now
and in the coming days.*

In Christ,

Timothy C. Tennent, PhD
President
Asbury Theological Seminary

A hand-written note adds, "What a legacy your personal and professional investment in Asbury and Spring Arbor has been. Our prayers are with you."

15. Billy Graham

My long association with the Reverend Billy Graham goes back to 1953. The Christian Broadcasting Association (CBA) was founded by servicemen who had experience with Moody Radio. Their ministry in Hawaii consisted of buying time to broadcast Christian content on one of the three AM stations out there.

In January of 1950, Charles Palmquist, one of the servicemen who had married a girl from Bronson, Michigan, came to the radio station in Coldwater. He was seeking work because the stations in Hawaii had kicked off all Christian broadcasting. The servicemen were no longer allowed to buy time on those stations.

At that time, I operated and partially owned WTVB radio station in Coldwater. I hired Charles as an air-time salesman, and from him I learned about the situation in Hawaii. They had tried and failed to get a permit for their own station, and I was brash enough to say, "Well, let me have a try at it."

So I was able to get a permit from the FCC for the CBA and established the first full-service FM broadcast station in Hawaii, although there was a little 10-watt station at the Punahoe School.

The CBA station in Hawaii went on the air in 1953 and realized exceptional coverage, even in the lee of the mountains. Honolulu is on the south and southwest side of Oahu, and there's a sizable residential community across the Koolau range of mountains.

Right from the outset we had a considerable audience and made an immediate market for the new, high-fidelity receivers. By broadcasting such quality programming as the Honolulu Symphony Orchestra, we obtained an almost instant audience. And of course we featured a great deal of Christian music.

Cornelius Keur, prior to his going into the military, had worked at Moody Bible Institute. He became involved in developing the program called "Songs in the Night" with a young pastor from the Village Church in Western Springs, Illinois, named Billy Graham. And by the way, the station I built, owned, and operated in Coldwater was one of the first stations outside of Chicago to air "Songs in the Night," which I was broadcasting by 1954.

The Billy Graham Association had offices in Australia serving their ministries in southern Asia—Billy had begun his crusade ministry in 1947 in Los Angeles which hosted the first big crusade. When Billy traveled between Australia and the United States, he had to deal with that 13-hour time difference coming half-way around the world—and of course that was back before jet planes, so he was making the journey in the old prop planes.

Billy would stop for a week in Hawaii to allow his biological clock to catch up, and during that week he scheduled meetings with the evangelical ministers and always had a press conference or two. I attended those news conferences and got to know him in the late

1950s, and then in 1960 the radio branch of BGEA was getting underway with their stations in North Carolina.

The CBA was struggling financially, and Billy was out in Hawaii the same time I was, so he connected with the CBA board and agreed to take over the defacto control of CBA which involved KAIM radio, both AM and FM. Billy's involvement made it possible to make very definite improvements in equipment and coverage.

One early meeting when Billy was coming back from the Far East was held at the Long House on Waikiki Beach (now replaced by a high rise building). We had 20 or 25 evangelical ministers there, and right next to me was a little guy no more than 5'6" tall, possibly a Christian and Missionary Alliance missionary to Polynesia. He could hardly wait for the comment time, and when that time came—Billy was at the end of the table, I was right next to him, and the missionary was right next to me—the little guy popped out of his chair and said, "There are 20 thousand islands in Polynesia where there is no Christian witness, and if you were to spend one day on each island, it would take you 60 years to reach them all."

Billy turned to me and said, "Harold, we've got to do something about that."

The upshot was that we put in the most powerful AM station ever built in Hawaii, 50,000 watts, with the signal directed into Polynesia, and operating on a frequency that fit between the channels used in both Australia and Japan, so it was essentially a clear channel. Because of that station during its period of operation under BGEA, we heard from all over the world because we literally had worldwide coverage.

Actually, Hawaii is the uttermost part of the earth from Jerusalem, so when Jesus instructed his disciples to go to the ends of the earth, that was Hawaii. I once had a map centered on Hawaii that showed the various distances around the world, and Jerusalem was farthest away. Take a globe and study it and you'll see that's true. So that is how I got involved with Billy Graham.

My continuing involvement on Billy's Blue Ridge Broadcasting board involved WMIT, an FM station that went silent. It was licensed at Black Mountain, NC, and BGEA bought it before I joined the board in 1960. Billy was chair of the board and Bev Shea, Cliff Barrows, and T. W. Wilson were some of the other board members. With its location atop Klingman's Dome on the flank of Mount Mitchell, its coverage was a six-state area, one of the largest in the United States of any FM station.

Regulations at that time demanded that you have an operator on duty at all times. We built an apartment up there on the mountain, and the operator would go up in November and not return to normal civilization until the snow and ice melted in February. The elevation of the antenna is a mile above sea level, so there's a lot of ice and snow. The distance from the studio to the transmitter is less than 10 miles, but the driving distance is 40 miles.

At the time I came on the board they were subsidizing the station to the tune of about $300,000 a year. As secretary/treasurer, my immediate objective with the BRB was to make it self-supporting, and then go beyond that. We built a substantial audience for Christian programming to the point where today, not only is it self-supporting, but we also support a 24/7 satellite signal that blankets North Africa from Morocco to Cairo with Arabic Christian programming, and we have distributed many thousands of fixed-tune satellite receivers to followers of Christ. We don't give details because the radicals would dearly love to quash that ministry.

Also, two or three times during the year, we'll run a day urging the support of a worthy ministry. Last October, in one day, Blue Ridge Broadcasting raised $616,000 for a particular ministry. We also play a big role in the Christmas Shoebox campaign, and we're very active civically. A year or two ago we distributed emergency counseling packets to several thousand police and other first call interveners including Bibles and other materials, and we have a total community impact. We've long since contributed back to the mother organization much more than the funding they provided to us at the outset.

Right now, the project before I got sick was to replace our twin 25-year-old transmitters. That whole project will cost about $400,000. This is no financial challenge because I include funded depreciation in the budget—something rarely done in religious organizations. We put aside in a designated reserve an amount equal to the depreciation of the equipment each year as part of the budget. This is just common sense so that when the new equipment fails, we can write a check for the needed upgrade.

BRB is headquartered in the Cove in Asheville, and we also house the servers supporting the BGEA. BRB is currently chaired by David Bruce, Billy Graham's personal assistant. Bruce and his wife were married in the Dearborn Free Methodist Church. She is a registered nurse who cared for Ruth Graham during her lingering illness before she passed away.

Note: The above information on Billy Graham was dictated February 1, 2016, as Dad waited at the hospital for his third radiation treatment for inoperable pancreatic cancer. After returning home, we looked on his shelves and found Billy's book *Facing Death: And the Life After* (Minneapolis, MN: Grason, 1987). The flyleaf has this message and autograph written in green ink:

> *"To my faithful brother Harold Munn. God bless and keep you always. Billy Graham. Mar. 15, '88. 1 Cor. 15:58."*
>
> *That Bible text reads, "Therefore, my beloved, be steadfast, immovable, always excelling in the work of the Lord, because you know that in the Lord your labor is not in vain."*

— The End —

Appendix

A Time to be Born, A Time to Die

"For everything that happens in life—there is a season, a right time for everything under heaven: A time to be born, a time to die"

—Ecclesiastes 3:1-2a (The Voice).

Obituary

Earle Harold Munn Jr, age 87, of Parma, MI, died of complications from pancreatic cancer at his home. He was the son of Earle Harold and Luella Mae (Asfahl) Munn. Born Sept 7, 1928, in Vandalia, IL, Hal is survived by his wife, C. Ella (Bronson), sons H. Derwin, M. Douglas, and daughter M. Renée Runyon; five grandchildren, seven great grandchildren, and many nieces and nephews.

Hal received his Federal Communications Commission (FCC) first class radio license at age 14 and in 1947 at age 17 became a lifetime member of the Institute of Electrical and Electronic Engineers (IEEE), the world's largest professional organization of any scientific profession. The following year he graduated from Hillsdale College, Hillsdale, MI, with a degree in physics plus many credits in chemistry and mathematics. He taught high school for one year in North Adams and one year at Pittsford before starting WTVB-WANG radio stations in Coldwater. Other stations he established and owned include Ypsilanti (WYSI), Hillsdale (WBSE), and Sturgis (WSTR).

In addition to radio, he was a pioneer in broadband communications, received one of the three first cable TV permits awarded by the FCC, and started many cable companies including Coldwater and Columbia Cablevision.

In 1950, Hal established the E. Harold Munn Jr. and Associates Broadcast Engineering Consulting firm and in that capacity built or consulted with about 800 radio stations in all 50 states and nearly 70 colleges and universities.

Two notable examples are Bell Broadcasting Corporation in Detroit, the first FCC-approved African American-owned radio station in the United States providing a foundation for the Motown music industry, and a 50,000 watt AM station in Hawaii for the Billy Graham Evangelistic Association that broadcast a Christian witness to 20,000 Polynesian islands and literally around the world.

In 2005, Hal was inducted into the Michigan Broadcasting Hall of Fame. He served as a trustee and in many administrative capacities with the following organizations: Coldwater Board of Public Utilities from 1960—1995 and president of that board beginning in 1967; from 1960—2015 on the board of the Blue Ridge Broadcasting Corporation, a listener-supported ministry of the Billy Graham Evangelistic Association; from 1960—2010 as a trustee of Spring Arbor University; and from 1983—2015 as a trustee of Asbury Theological Seminary, Wilmore, KY. Since childhood Hal was a member of the Free Methodist Church and served that denomination in many volunteer administrative capacities from 1950—2015.

Acknowledgments

My own father died in 1981, yet when I married Hal Munn's daughter, Renée, in 1983, the last thing on my mind was the prospect of gaining another dad. Yet, there he was, a wise and kind father-in-law who never gave advice unless asked, who never said an unkind word about me, and who even asked for and often took my advice—right down to his last days.

I can't repay him, but out of gratitude I jotted down *Storehouses of Snow*, the documentary of our adventures together in Antarctica. He was pleased with that book, and he took delight in the drafts he saw of this book as well.

In his final days, few things brought Dad more enjoyment than the opportunity to reminisce. I'd sit by his recliner in the living room, and then in a chair by his bed, and write down whatever he said. Editing such transcriptions is like boiling down maple sap—it takes a lot of time and energy and must be allowed to simmer—but I think you'll find the 10 percent that remains is sweet and good. This is my tribute to him, to his beloved wife, and to his legacy.

Initial inspiration came from the Rev. Tom Ball, PhD, a key player in developing the Spring Arbor University department of communications and media and whose spiritual and professional journey was ignited and mentored by Hal Munn.

"Dan," he said, "you've got to write his biography!"

That seed sprouted after a conversation I had with Dr. Grant Wacker of Duke University Divinity School, the biographer who wrote *America's Pastor: Billy Graham and the Shaping of a Nation* (Harvard UP, Cambridge: 2014).

"Have you ever heard of Harold Munn?" I asked Dr. Wacker.

"I can't say that I have," he replied.

That was on Sunday, January 31, 2016, at a Hillsdale College lecture. On Monday during our trip to the hospital for yet another radiation treatment, I asked Dad to tell me the story of his association with Billy Graham. The following day, I printed out that story and handed it to Dr. Wacker when I saw him again. Such a noble life should not be left in the shadows.

That first interview with Dad led to another, and another, just snatches of time here and there until suddenly this little volume came together with the same haste as his perpetual filings with the FCC. The deadline was literal—to get it written and printed in time to hand out at Dad's memorial service.

As an investigative journalist, it unnerves me to publish without verification the many facts, dates, and figures printed here. Please receive them for what they are—parting thoughts from a man whose encyclopedic memory is slipping away in his final days.

Thanks to Spring Arbor University for academic leeway to make time for this project, and thanks to copy editing students Hannah Blume, Nathaniel Bortz, Madeline Hooker,

Brianna Loomis, Alexa Matthews, and Simon Reidsma for their blitz-proofing.

My wife, Renée, read and critiqued a draft of this manuscript, and David McKenna graciously provided valuable factual corrections and stylistic suggestions.

I accept responsibility for the inevitable goofs. As it stands, you have a frank and penetrating look into the mind and spirit of a devoted servant of Jesus—my second Dad, mentor, and friend: E. Harold Munn Jr.

—*Dan Runyon*

Made in the USA
Middletown, DE
20 March 2016